10 95

Tree Tales & Logging Trails

Gerald Ely Sarff

Gerald E. "Red" Sarff

I dedicate this book to my daughter Fonda Lynn.

Without her help and research

this book would not have been.

Forward

After spending two years in the Navy at Farragut Naval Base, about 26 miles south of Sandpoint, I fell in love with north Idaho and decided to make it home for me and my family.

In 1946 I moved to Sandpoint and started the Pend Oreille Sport Shop.

One of my early customers was a true outdoorsman by the name of Gerald E. (Red) Sarff. Red was a LOGGER, Hunter, sports fisherman, huckleberry picker and buyer.

Red came into the store quite often and we became good friends, through our mutual love for the mountains, lakes and streams of north Idaho and Alaska.

Mr. Sarff has done an excellent job of covering his adventures and experiences through his poems in this book. The poetry is written in plain English and so well that I could visualize each action or experience as I read them.

Mr. Sarff's knowledge of the mountains, woods and wildlife comes through loud and clear in all of his poems. They cover a bit of history and many of his experiences so well that I can visualize seeing the action in person.

Red with his wife Barb, until her passing in 1994, shared adventures as varied as huckleberry picking and commercial fishing. They have been lifelong supporters of sport fishing, elk and deer hunting. Their love for North Idaho and Alaska comes through in Red's poetry.

His poems brought to mind many pleasant memories to me. I recommend this book of interesting poems to you without reservations.

—Don W. Samuelson
Governor of Idaho 1967-1971

Tree Tales and Logging Trails

A tree don't talk like you or me
It isn't everyone that can talk to a tree
When you read this book keep an open mind
And be sure to read between the lines.

A few words *from the* Author

Jack says talking to trees is lots of fun
That trees will talk to anyone
He also says that trees can see
They have better eyes than you or me

Jack says that a tree has many ears
And it remembers everything it hears
He says that a tree can communicate
With any tree, from any state

Jack thinks he's dumb but I think he's smart
He knows proper logging is really an art
He asked me to write this book
It's amazing just how long it took

This book is fictional but many things are true
The judgement of which is left up to you
Old or young, big or small
We hope this book is enjoyed by all

Love our forests, enjoy our land
Give Mother Nature a helping hand
We can do better than what's been done
Taking care of our land should be number one

So set back, relax, and read for a spell
Imagine a few things that a tree could tell
There are stories that will make you smile
That alone will make this book worthwhile

Jack

Years ago I was born on this farm
I helped my Dad build the new barn
I've milked many cows and put up tons of hay
But logging's the reason that we've made it pay

My folks worked hard and they did quite well
Now they've moved in to town, to rest a spell
I've worked as a Logger most of my life
While the farm's been handled by the kids and my wife

Our Daughter's getting married this coming fall
Our twins are off playing professional ball
I'll take pad and pencil and sit by the brook
For I've got the day off and I'll work on this book

Now every one knows that a tree can't walk
But how many know that a tree can talk
It's true they can't talk like you or me
And it's not every one that can talk to a tree

When you walk through a forest enjoy the trees
Don't be ashamed to say "Thank You and Please"
Ask the trees questions, you don't need to be shy
You've nothing to lose, give it a try

I've been talking to trees for forty years or more
But haven't written down what they've said before
Writing it down will take a long time
Because most of the trees talk in rhyme

Birth *of a* Tree

A tree is a marvel to behold
But some at a hundred years are old
There is nothing lovelier than a tree
And not many things wiser one can see

God made trees soon after he made the land
They're nearly as old as the wind and sand
Some trees were here long before
There ever was a Dinosaur

I am certain that God had a plan
When he put trees all over the land
He knew that all he would ever need
Was to scatter out a little seed

The seed would sprout and the trees would grow
Then their seed would scatter to and fro
God will always do his best
And Mother Nature does the rest

It's just my opinion, for what it is worth
Billions of seeds are scattered over the earth
Seeds that are several centuries old
Can sprout and grow or so I've been told

If someone says a forest won't ever grow back
You know there is some experience he lacks
Timber is something that all of us need
A tree was cut to make this book you read

Clear Cutting is one thing I've seldom approved
I prefer taking only timber that should be removed
But I once saw a patch stripped as clean as a bone
Nothing was left but some brush and some stone

Four years later there were trees everywhere
When trees grow that thick we call it Dog Hair
About thirty years later I chanced to drive by
The trees were thinned out and a hundred feet high

The Fir *and the* Kid

See that Fir tree down by the well
There's many a story he can tell
We first met when I was a kid
And let me tell you what I did

When I was nine my Dad said he could
Teach me how to cut firewood
This might be something that I shouldn't tell
I took Dad's ax and went down by the well

I thought my Dad would be proud of me
If I could cut down a firewood tree
I saw a big root sticking out of the ground
I chopped at it and thought I heard a sound

I laid down the ax and looked everywhere
But I saw no one but the tree standing there
Since there was no one around that I could see
I wondered if the noise had come from the tree

I started to chop at it some more
And that old tree let out a roar
He said clearly "Wouldn't you know
You just cut a nick in my big toe"

I dropped the ax and started to cry
That big old tree let out a sigh
"I was just kidding, don't you bawl
I hardly felt that nick at all"

I said "I'm sorry, I'll get rid of the ax
Down in the well so you can relax"
The big tree replied, "No don't do that
Your Dad needs his ax, he's a good Lumberjack"

"Your Dad has worked hard at cleaning this farm
He has cut down trees that were doing it harm
He has built a house and also a barn
All from the trees that grew on this farm"

"When your Dad cuts down a tree he plants a few back
For that is one sign of a good Lumberjack
When he thins out the woods the younger trees grow
But as you can see I'm not ready to go"

That big tree had much more to say
But it would wait for another day
He said "Head home and you might want to hurry
If the ax is found missing your folks will worry"

I didn't know a tree could talk
Hearing him was quite a shock
I didn't know a tree could feel
I hoped that nick was quick to heal

He said that bump hadn't hurt at all
And he was sorry that he made me bawl
That big tree and I have become very good friends
The stories he's told are in the thousand of tens

I've learned a lot about all kinds of trees
They like hot weather and hate a cold freeze
They like a cool breeze but hate strong winds
It strips off their leaves and even breaks limbs

Water and sunshine help make them grow
Some in the winter enjoy the snow
Some fear insects, some fear disease
But fire worries all of the trees

By the well

Once he told me how he came to be here
And that was back about 40 some year
For many long years he just lay as a seed
In order to sprout there were things he would need

He said "I was afraid I'd be Squirrel feed
But I'd rather be that than just be a weed"
He said "A guy came and cleared a little land
And built a small shack about where you stand"

"He dug the well beside the shack
And built a Still a ways out back"
My Mom told me once she remembered it well
She can still recall that fermenting smell

"To build the shack he leveled the ground
And doing that scattered us seeds all around
In his hurry the dirt did fly
I was thrown on an old cow pie"

"If the rain did come and the sun did shine
I knew I'd sprout if given time
By early June the ground was warm
And not much later I was born"

"A lot of us seed became trees that year
I was larger than most, soon able to hear
Part of the reason I was larger than most
Was that my roots were growing in rich compost"

"Several years later on a cold winter day
The Law Men came out and took him away
Soon after that they tore it all down
Only us trees and the well were left around"

Back then making moonshine was called doing wrong
But he started a Fir tree that's healthy and strong
To trees moonshine would never taste good
But good ol' well water tastes just like it should

Cedar

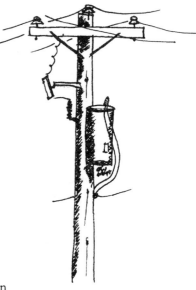

That Fir tree sure can see and hear
He always knows when I am near
He always greets me with a "Hi"
As do the Cedars that grow nearby

Cedars are very lovely trees
They're always willing to talk to me
To Cedar trees I'll give a toast
I've made a lot of Cedar posts

A Cedar is a tree which doesn't complain
He doesn't mind the heat he doesn't mind the rain
He grows in the swamps and on the hills
In his boughs may nest some Whip-or-Wills

A Cedar told me he'd like to be cut
That he was getting a rotten butt
He asked me to make him into a pole 80 feet long
And he asked me to do it while he was still strong

I cut that tree the very next year
The rest of his family sure did cheer
His Grandpa said "I'm proud of that Grandson of mine
From now on he'll be supporting a power line"

Then he told me something that I understood
Trees should be cut while they're still good
Since they've been serving life for millions of years
He said being cut was the least of their fears

He said "For years I've been ready to go
But there was one thing I want to know
Why all the Loggers would give me the eye
Then shake their heads and walk on by"

I talked to that Cedar quite a lot
The Loggers all knew that he had rot
He didn't want to just stand there and die
He told me this with a tear in his eye

Then he said "Why don't they give me a break
They know I'd make a lot of good shakes"
He said "I'm bigger than most trees on the coast
I'd probably make over a thousand good posts"

I told him to relax not feel so blue
I said "I'll see what I can do"
I got permission but had to do the right thing
And I wasn't to cut him in summer or spring

To get permission to cut that Cedar down
I had to create a plan that was sound
Because of a creek I had to take care
To dirty the water I wouldn't dare

The Ecologist said he had a doubt
That I could skid that big Cedar out
The Forest Service said there had been a mistake
That Cedar would make too much shake

There was one thing that they didn't know
I had two horses and would wait for snow
I waited 'til the snow got just right
Then got out of bed before day light

I hitched up the black and hitched up the gray
And headed up the hill about the break of day
I picked a good spot for the Cedar to go
And I laid him down gently in the deep soft snow

I didn't harm any trees or hurt the ground
And as for the creek I just went out around
I didn't have to cross the creek or hurt any Trout
In just one day I skidded that Big Cedar out

Now I have a lot of shakes to put on the barn
And several hundred posts to use on the farm
For that old tree he didn't rot away
He's part of this farm to this very day

Grow a Tree

One tree said while talking to me
"It don't take a lot to grow a tree
There's lots of seed on the forest floor
Some has been there a hundred years or more"

"We do best when you thin us out
It lets light in so seed can sprout"
That's always made sense to me
So I told him I sure did agree

I've asked trees questions over the years
And some of their answers would burn your ears
If you get a tree started he'll talk a long time
Every thing he says will be in rhythm and rhyme

Elk Romance

High in the mountains where the grass grows green
There is a meadow where the Elk can be seen
Along one side runs a cool clear crick
Along its' banks the brush grows thick

In the middle of the meadow grows a large old Pine
Where once was dumped a lot of salt brine
I've sat in that Pine on a limb that was thick
To take pictures of Elk as they work the salt lick

I've sat in that tree till late at night
To photograph the Elk bulls as they fight
I've taken some pictures early in the morn'
Of the cow Elk as their calves are being born

That old Pine knows when Elk are near
He knows the difference between Elk and Deer
That old Pine sure does a lot of laughin'
Once he told me what he just saw happen

There was a Bull, two Cows and a Calf
It was the Bull that made him laugh
There was a young Bull standing near by
And he was giving those Cows the eye

The old Bull got mad and pawed the ground
And proceeded to chase the young Bull around
He ran that young Bull plum over the hill
But when he got back the meadow was still

While he was gone the Cows did stray
And another Bull stole those Cows away
He really got mad and his eyes turned red
But the tree wouldn't repeat what he had said

He took after his Cows on a dead run
To show that Cow Stealer who was number one
Now hear that bugle and hear the reply
You can bet that old Bull has blood in his eye

He'll take back the Cows and add a few more
He'll take a few extra to even the score
The tree told me he loves fall best of all
To hear the Bulls bugle and hear the Cows call

A White Pine's Opinion *and* More

I go hunting nearly every year
About a hundred miles south of here
I pitch my tent near a huge White Pine
That tree is now a good friend of mine

He's so old he's turning blue
But he claims that isn't true
That White Pine is taller than the rest
In his top there's an Eagle's nest

He says he has a hole in one side
It's a place where the Squirrels can hide
He said they pack in lots of fireweed
To build their nests and eat the seed

He tells me where the Deer hang out
And when the stream is full of Trout
He can tell me where to find a Buck
And always knows when I've had luck

He tells me how silly the Tree Huggers are
They're always coming from near and far
They come around about twice a year
He doubts that some of them can hear

They always have a pencil, a pad and a tape
They measure him and guess his weight
They drill new holes in his trunk
To see if he has grown or shrunk

"Some of them don't know a lot
They don't even know that I have rot
But one guy that wore a dark hard hat
Was the only one who would argue back"

"The other said he was the Boss
And he didn't care about lumber loss
He said the birds light in that tree
That makes it more valuable to you and me"

The guy in the hard hat said "That's absurd
There are plenty of trees for every bird"
He said "Birds have wings and they can fly
They can build their nests in trees near by"

That hard hatted guy sure argued back
He'd spent some time as a Lumberjack
He'd worked for years and been around
He could tell you if a tree was sound

He'd worked in mills and gone to school
With what he knows he's nobody's fool
When he's the boss it gets done right
Give him any guff and you have a fight

I filled my tag early and had lots of time
So I talked some more with the old White Pine
We talked of things we hadn't before
He talked to me about the Civil War

He said the Battle of Gettysburg was a terrible fight
They fought for three days and for three nights
Cannon fire caused trees to fall all around
The Corn fields were flattened to the ground

He mentioned the Shenandoah and the Battle of Shilo
Where the bullets were flying thicker than snow
Peach trees in bloom, there was spring in the air
But too many young men were falling every where

That old tree has told me things from the past
He never fails to answer a question I've asked
He said that he could remember when
Our country was run by honorable men

Abraham Lincoln was such a man
He ran the country with an even hand
But he didn't count honor in fighting a war
He'd earned his honor in the years before

I told that old White Pine I'd like to know where
He got all his knowledge since he hadn't been there
He said "We trees talk to each other all over this land
I'm sure that is something that you understand"

While I packed my camp the next morning to go
He mentioned something he thought I should know
He said "There's a plan for building a road
For hauling out trees by the truck load"

I prayed the logging would be done right
That enough would be cut to let in the light
There were many trees the wind had blown down
That should come out to clear the ground

On the way back home I thought of a plan
With that timber being on Federal land
And me on the list to receive by mail
A form to bid on that timber sale

When that form came I would fill it out
If I got the job I'd have no doubt
I'd pledge whatever it might take
The job would be done without a mistake

Going to Work

I was home that very next day
And checked what the Forest Service had to say
They said it would be a good sized sale
And I'd get a bid form in the mail

They wanted the logging started that fall
But they didn't have a plan to take it all
They had a little road to build
And one low spot to be filled

From what I heard they had a good plan
And I was sure I knew the Lay-Out man
If I remembered right his name was Thor
I'd worked on a job with him before

I had some work to do on the farm
Giving my wife a break would do no harm
I told her she should rest a spell
I'd fix the gate and patch the well

The hay was already in the shed
Close to where the stock would be fed
I'd cleaned the garden the other day
But still had fruit trees to dormant spray

When I finally had some leisure time
I spent it with that wife of mine
I talked with my friend down by the well
He always has a few more stories to tell

It talked to me

After dinner I read the news
Sometimes lay back to take a snooze
But this evening I felt something in the air
My daughter Sal, had something to share

Sal said "Daddy I know that you just ate
But I've something to tell you that just won't wait
I took your advice and tried talking to a tree
And he actually did talk back to me"

"It was your friend down by the well
Now I also think that he is swell
I wish I'd talked to him before
I'm going to talk to him some more"

"I was down by the well when I heard a shout
I wondered what it was all about
I heard the tree clearly say
'Talk to me, it'll make my day' "

"To talk to you I've been trying for years
I commenced to think you didn't have ears"
"I told him my name was Sal
I knew he was my Dad's pal"

"We talked for an hour or more
Before I had to do my chores
Now you know I have no more doubt
What your talking to trees is all about"

To land a job

About that time I answered the phone
And some one asked if I was home
The guy said his name was Thor
That I had worked for him before

Thor said he'd talked to a guy named Rob
Who had been talking to me about a job
Rob said you hoped to get that sale
And were expecting to hear by mail

He asked me if I had turned in a bid
On the timber sale up Turnip Ridge
I said I was still waiting for the form
He replied "You better see me in the morn"

He asked if I could see him at 8 o'clock
He wanted us to have a talk
He said "This is something that won't wait
Just meet me at the Ranger Station gate"

I met him there and I was glad I did
Cause if I hadn't I'd missed that bid
Thor said "That sale is very soon
I understand it's this afternoon"

Well I wondered how that could be
Since no one had bothered to notify me
Once your name is on the mailing list
It's hard to be accidentally missed

I asked him why he didn't bid on it too
He said "No I'd rather leave it up to you
But you might not think I'm being nice
If you get that job there will be a price"

He explained he cruised timber only part of the time
That he could run Jammer or Dozer or even pull line
I said "No you should be the main Boss
That way there won't be any timber loss"

We talked it all over and laid out a bid
I took his advice and I am glad that I did
The papers were finished none too soon
We won the bid that afternoon

But the Head Ranger got a little sore
Saying "You wouldn't have it if not for Thor"
I told him that he sure was right
If not for Thor there'd have been a fight

The Ranger said "There's a man, whose name is Bob
He'll be Environmentalist over your job
If he's not satisfied he'll give you trouble
Chances are he'll break your bubble"

A Logger's Tale

In just one week we'd hired Rob
And five more men do to the job
Our camp was set up, the equipment in place
One might have thought we were running a race

The very first day that we started the job
A guy drove up saying his name was Bob
I said "You'll need to talk to the Boss of this show
Thor can tell you what you need to know"

"Any complaints then talk to me
Any suggestions well we'll see
We'll work together on this job
You, me and Thor, and Sawyer Rob"

We spent two days just walking around
He couldn't tell if a tree was sound
At first he was ready to disagree
About every cut and every tree

I could have gotten angry at his attitude
If I hadn't been in a darn good mood
I said "Relax, slow down a spell
Thor has marked the trees to be fell"

He said "First tell me, so I will know
Why Thor marked that healthy Fir to go"
I replied "It happens to be a rotten Hemlock
Listen to the sound when you give it a knock"

There were trees leaning across a brook
Bob said "We'll have to go by the book
So the stream won't fill with sand
We'll have to leave those trees stand"

I said "I know there's knowledge that I lack
But a line around them will pull them back"
He bet me a dollar it couldn't be done
But I showed him how with the very first one

It's not such a difficult thing you see
To guide the direction of a falling tree
Just notch the side where you want it to go
Then force the tree that direction you know

Climb the tree as high as you are able
Then set a choker and hook the cable
A Skidder or Jammer will do the rest
And a slow steady pull will work the best

We didn't disturb the bank or stream
We left it running clear and clean
I could see that Bob was quite impressed
When Rob left a tree with an Eagle's nest

We worked over every foot of ground
Taking the trees that were not sound
We took old trees that were getting weak
Leaving young ones growing around their feet

We took about half the timber off that land
Now on that ground there's a healthy stand
If all the forests were logged that way
There would never be a forest that faded away

Bob learned a lot about logging every day
And how easy it was to log the right way
He learned how to skid and how to fall
Turned out he wanted to learn it all

When Thor came down with the flu
And the Choker Setter had it too
We asked Bob if he'd fill in
He had some vacation time coming to him

The weather held and with the men's skill
Soon a million feet were hauled to the mill
In two more weeks the job was done
We worked hard but had lots of fun

I hated to let all the men go
Especially since there wasn't much snow
Thor and I and Sawyer Rob
Worked a week cleaning up the job

I moved my equipment back to the farm
And stored the Dozer in the barn
I kept the Skidder ready to go
Because I use it plowing snow

All the men got a week's bonus pay
I hoped to hire them again some day
Then I took them all out to dine
Even the wives had a good time

Law and Order

One day my friend down by the well
Said he had something important to tell
He said "The Law came by yesterday
Though they didn't have a lot to say"

He said "I knew what they were looking for
Because two guys were here the night before
Those guys buried something in a box
And I bet it wasn't filled with rocks"

"I told the Law Men where to go see
But they didn't hear, me being a tree
They looked around then looked some more
I wondered if they knew what for"

"Now you see that large Vine Maple clump
Behind it you will find a hump
Beneath the hump you'll find a stash
And in the stash you'll find some cash"

He said "Call the Law and have them come out
And you can be their private scout"
He said "Those guys didn't look too bright
You can nab them both all right"

The tree told me and I told them
Before sunset the Law was back again
Those guys came back that very night
We grabbed them both without a fight

We caught them because of that Fir tree
And all because he could talk to me
But the Lawmen never truly knew
Who supplied the important clue

To cut a tree

One tree had this to say
"You can take me down any day
You cut the grass and pull the weeds
And they too start from little seeds"

"God planted a lot of grass
It was good, it fed the Ass
He planted fruits, herbs and weeds
They were all just little seeds"

"He planted seed which became trees
Created them in wondrous varieties
He put me here or so I understand
To serve all creatures including men"

"I've been feeding Squirrels, Birds and Bees
My seed cones are piled up to my knees
If you cut me down, haul me out
More of my offspring could sprout"

One tree said, as I was walking by
"I'd rather be cut than to stand here and die
Make me into a house, barn or shed
If I'm of use I'm not really dead"

An old Oak said "I love all man
I want to serve any way I can
I think that I can help you more
If I become a hardwood floor"

There was a Birch tree standing near
He said "I would make some good Veneer
If you want use my bark too
Haven't you heard of a Birch Canoe?"

A coastal tree living near a farm
Said "The Owls prefer living in the barn
They don't need me any more
They never needed me before"

There was an old tree that was very tall
He had the best answers of them all
"Take those of us that you need
Leaving the rest to make more seed"

"Thin us out to let in more light
Taking the old, to do it right
But leave the young so they can grow
Taking them is senseless don't you know"

One tree said "I am being spurned
I'm to be left or so I learned
To leave me stand is doing wrong
I'd make good lumber while I'm still strong"

He said "My Grandpa's standing over there
With his bark falling off and limbs so bare
I wish you'd take him if you could
While he's still good for firewood"

"Some of my offspring often complain
They don't get enough sun or enough rain
To let my offspring get their fill
Cut me down and haul me to a mill"

He said "Then there's that political plan
To lock millions of acres into wilderness land
In wilderness there's no access
So fighting fire has little success"

Common Sense

I read something in the paper the other day
About some Attorney down Boise way
You ought to have heard her scream and shout
The Forestry wants to take some burned timber out

The Sierra Club called it a "Fragile Fire"
Their reasons and wording I can't admire
They say it may have been started by man
And now the river will fill with sand

The Attorney says that will kill some Salmon
And that of course would cause a famine
Well I've seen Mother Nature go to work
And fill whole darned rivers full of dirt

The attorney says don't cut anything down
To me that kind of thinking isn't sound
They won't accept anything I say
But I'm going to say it anyway

Remove all the scorched timber and debris
And start it again with newly planted trees
Seed the river banks with Clover and Grass
Soon you'll be fishing for Salmon and Bass

This is what the Forest Service said
"We need money to stabilize the watershed"
The land would heal many years faster
That would make it a smaller disaster

The Wise Old Owl

I visited my brother out on the coast
Did some fishing and made some posts
Had lots of fun, I shouldn't complain
But that type of fishing just isn't my game

I heard the ocean fishing had gone to pot
The Environmentalists had the logging stopped
They'll say the Loggers have cut every tree
And it's bare as far as the eye can see

They'll tell you the forest will never grow back
But they're not fooling this old Lumberjack
I can show you photos of fields once bare
Look at them now, there's timber there

The old Spotted Owl has no place to rest
They have no place to build their nest
But I've heard those Owls moved to the farm
And now they're nesting in a barn

We should be so smart

When I was in Alaska panning for gold
I talked to trees both young and old
One tree stated I was the only one
That he'd ever met who knew their tongue

Once he said "Look over there
And you'll see a Grizzly Bear
You see that great big Sitka Spruce
That's where Bear often ambush Moose"

"They'll hide behind that tree and peek
And pick a moose that's fat and sleek
I've seen one Bear that has the skill
To always make a perfect kill"

"But now the Moose are scarce 'round here
And the Bear have turned to killing Deer
They wander now that snow capped hill
And are finding lots of Goats to kill"

"Just walk along that stream of cold clear water
You'll see some Bear tracks and spot some Otter
But stick around till the Salmon run
You'll see dozens of Bear not just one"

I learned many things from that old tree
But decided there wasn't where I wanted to be
And that I might just loose my hair
If soon I didn't get out of there

Gold *and* Eagle

Once I was told about a stream
Where I could find that golden sheen
But all the gold that I could find
Was not enough to make a dime

Since I had walked in some twenty mile
I talked to the trees to make the trip worthwhile
They had Bear stories they wanted to tell
And many others that I liked as well

A Cedar tree said "Look way up high
See that Eagle soaring in the sky
And in my top you'll spot her nest
With three little Eagles breast to breast"

"You should be here when the Salmon run
Those Eagles sure do have some fun
You'll see lots of Bear, large and small
And you might just hear a lone Wolf call"

"Soon after that the Bear will den
That's when the fighting will really begin
I tell you the Wolves howl all night
They're always trying to pick a fight"

"This is the winter feeding ground
And Moose come here from miles around
Though there aren't as many as there used to be
But there will still be dozens for you to see"

"Wolves pull a Moose down when they want to eat
About all they leave are bones and feet
When the night is cold and the moon is bright
A pack of Wolves are quite a sight"

"When the snow is laying four feet deep
You'll think the world is fast asleep
That's when the Mink and Martin get their fill
So that's when the Owl can make his kill"

That tree doesn't know I plan to go back
And build myself a strong winter shack
I'll build it back among the trees
And make it warm against the winter freeze

I plan to take along my wife
So she can photograph the wildlife
Photos of Mink, Martin and Arctic Owl
Pictures and tapes of the Wolves as they howl

We'll photograph Moose and Otter too
And hope to take pictures of Caribou
I plan on staying up late some nights
So maybe I can see the northern lights

To Do a Job Right

Since that time I've been back
Done some work on that shack
Did some hunting and got a Moose
And talked some more to the Sitka Spruce

But now I'm home and doing well
Think it's time to log a spell
I got a call from my friend Thor
He'd like to work with me some more

We talked quite a while on the phone
He'd been waiting for me to get home
Said he needed a helping hand
To do a job on Indian land

He said "The job could be quite good
There are millions of feet of good wood"
He said "This job could take awhile
I've driven through timber for many a mile"

The Tribal Council had a good plan
They chose Thor for their man
He wanted to do the best he could
To harvest their forest the way one should

We got together with the Tribe
Wanted to work with them, side by side
We met the leader of their land
And with him was his right hand man

We drove through thousands of acres of old trees
The Enviros said "Leave them for the Birds and Bees"
Well they have their plan
To take all timber away from man

Five thousand acres to be logged with sense
And a few brushy places to be fenced
Several areas had been logged before
And the logging practices were very poor

They'd left the rotten trees stand
And that's a detriment to the land
The stumps were cut high and small trees tore down
Long butts and tree tops all over the ground

Streams were filled with brush and debris
One stream was so muddy a fish couldn't breathe
We showed them a dozen things we could do
To make better hunting, fishing and hiking too

Thor made a plan that was something to see
I and the Indians were quick to agree
We planned to use their men when ever we could
They liked that and said it was good

The job was about 200 miles from home
And I don't like staying all alone
Asked my wife to stay part of the time
And to bring along her fishing line

Thor had paperwork he had to do
And with preparations I was busy too
We moved the equipment there in about one week
And set up our camp near a beautiful creek

Thor said "Get a hold of Sawyer Rob
And hire two men who will stay on the job
Start them sawing on the south hill
The section with the worst Beetle kill"

We talked it over and decided I should
Take two men, the Dozer and do what we could
Below the north rim to put in some trails
So early next spring we could start without fail

We had two Dozers, two Jammers and three Skidders to run
We hired a dozen good locals and not all of them young
Some of those guys had worked in the woods
And the rest wanted to prove that they could

I wanted to log the way one should
The way Thor planned it sure sounded good
We would take the old growth and some of the young
And clean out the brush to let in the sun

Clear Cutting is one thing that rarely is good
But that Beetle killed hill is one that should
If left alone disease and insects will spread
And won't stop destroying till the whole forest is dead

We have been on this job for over two years
And the job we are doing is sure bringing cheers
We have cleared the old mess out of the streams
And I'm catching Trout in some of my dreams

There are thickets of brush both large and small
That we're trying to fence by next fall
We are not working at a hurricane pace
We're not trying to win any kind of a race

We harvest half the timber, sometimes more
And take all the dead trees from the forest floor
We cut and pile brush, though it is tough
Leveling off some areas that are too rough

We've roads and trails here and there
All of them used by the Deer, Elk and Bear
And the brushy places that we will fence
Will be left there for the animals' defense

The men were working hard and didn't complain
But now we were getting snow instead of rain
Thor asked me what we ought to do
He had already asked the crew

We'd worked two winters without a break
Some of the men wanted to fish the lake
Some of them wanted to hunt for meat
They were tired of no Venison to eat

I said "Why not shut the job down
And move the equipment into town
I know the equipment has done it's best
And all the men sure need a rest"

"There is some brake work to be done
One of the Jammers has a broken drum
Lots of spark plugs to be changed
And other things to be rearranged"

"Pulleys and blocks are getting wore
I know we'll need to get some more
There's a couple months work for two good men
Getting the equipment ready to work again"

"I know two Mechanics that worked at the mill
They're retired now but they have the skill
They may be a little old but are still good men
They're willing to help us any way that they can"

We closed the job down for the winter
And took every man out to dinner
We were able to give each a bonus too
That is something we always try to do

The village folk put on a celebration
To tell all the Loggers congratulations
It was at the party I asked Thor
If he could handle the winter's chore

"This is something I planned to ask ya
My wife and I want to go to Alaska
This time with my loving wife
To share the Alaska winter life"

"We've made a list of things we'll need
Clothes and supplies and books to read
We need to get there as soon as we could
I still have to cut our winter's wood"

"There is a Native Village down on the shore
I'd say from my cabin it's two miles or more
One of the men said he'd finish my shack
If he could live in it until I came back"

Alaska Vacation

Our boys are going to college now
So they won't be home much any how
Sal works in town in Finance
She can take care of the ranch

The driveway she may have to plow
But she's done that for years now
We will miss our Sal, each day more
But if she needs help she'll call Thor

We'd been planning the trip for over a year
It took a week to pack when the time drew near
We had boxes and bundles, suitcases and crates
All of them labeled with contents and weights

We had a shovel, an axe, a saw and winter boots
Cases of canned goods and lots of dried fruits
There were medicines and cameras and film galore
Should be enough for a year or more

We had enough bedding to keep an Elephant warm
Then I added two more cases of Corn
There were boxes of books, even some magazines
We'd use candles and flashlights but no Kerosene

We packed enough clothes to stay warm and dry
But I almost forgot the whiskey and rye
If I'd forgotten those I wouldn't feel right
I might need them for Snake or frost bite

We had an appointment with the plane
So we had to leave in the snow and rain
Sal rode along in the overloaded van
So she could drive it home again

On the morning of December 8th
We landed in Sitka one hour late
There was a charter plane standing by
We found the Pilot to be a nice guy

He wasn't sure if he could pack it all
Into his plane, it made quite a haul
I heard him over the radio phone
He made me think of a guy back home

"This is Jim calling Buttonhook Bay
How's the weather up there today?"
"Hi Jim, this is Buttonhook Bay
I think you better fly in right away"

"The weather right now is calm and clear
But tonight there's to be a storm I hear"
Jim replied "We'll take off right away
I'd like to get back home yet today"

In thirty minutes we were in the air
Believe you me there was no room to spare
There was no wind, just clear blue sky
And Jim didn't have to fly very high

When Buttonhook Bay first came into sight
Jim told Jan to look to her right
"You see that little one room shack
That was built by your husband Jack"

"Since he expects you to live in that
Do you now want me to turn on back"
I said "Hey I built it nice and warm
It's sheltered from the wind and storm"

Jan replied "It may look small
But Jack and I will have a ball"
Jim landed the plane along the shore
He'd done the same many times before

A small fishing fleet was tied to the dock
That time of year they don't fish a lot
On the dock was a welcoming crowd
And all the hellos were long and loud

Our stuff was unloaded in record time
But by the end the sky showed storm sign
Jim said he'd be back in a week or so
If Jan changed her mind and wanted to go

Buttonhook Bay

I had visited with the Tlingets before
They are good workers that's for sure
Soon we had all our gear moved into a shed
Behind the store where they keep extra sleds

In the store I found my wife
Drinking coffee and enjoying life
I realized I was hungry in the store
I hadn't had a meal since the day before

They fed us Moose meat and hot cinnamon bread
Smoked Salmon and coffee it was good to be fed
I told some men I'd give extra pay
If they would move our stuff today

Someone asked "Where are you moving to?"
I said "Why I thought you all knew
I plan on moving into that shack
The one I started about 3 years back"

The store keeper said, "That won't do
We're planning on taking better care of you
My son's out there, he's raising pups
But if you insist he'll give it up"

"We have a good place for you to stay
And you can take pictures every day
Beside this store there is a house
It's for you to live in with your spouse"

They are good people without a doubt
But I didn't want to put them out
But they would have it no other way
So in the village we decided to stay

The house was clean with lots of space
A screened in porch and a fire place
It had bottled gas and running water
And on the mantle a mounted Otter

The bath room was a little small
But much better than none at all
Jan was so happy she started to cry
And I too had a tear in my eye

The next day we went out in one of the boats
Watched Fishermen run lines and drop floats
They were after Halibut and Crab for their winter supply
And needed some extra for visitors that often stop by

They had Moose meat enough for a year
But seldom bothered taking Deer
They hunted Seal for trim for their coats
Or used the long hair from Billygoats

The boys were busy trapping Beaver and Mink
They also trapped Martin and occasionally a Lynx
We took lots of photos of all that they did
We wanted the pictures to show our own kids

We went sledding by the light of the moon
I knew that three months would end all too soon
We sat up with our cameras several nights
To photograph the Wolves in some of their fights

The northern lights often lit up the whole sky
Like huge waving rainbows they sure catch the eye
We went snow shoeing just to have fun
And to get a glimpse of the short living sun

The Spruce at Buttonhook Bay

I went for a walk along Buttonhook Bay
To hear what Alaskan trees had to say
I asked a Spruce tree how he liked living up here
He said "I love it especially this time of year"

"I can see a hundred miles away
To islands where Deer feed everyday
I like to watch the Seals swim
And watch the Fishermen coming in"

"I like to watch Eagles build their nests
And on my limbs they often rest"
That tree told of things very few of us know
He said "Eagles won't fly when it's 40 below"

He said "In the winter the snow gets deep
It's always warm on my trunk and feet
And when my roots are nice and warm
I can endure any arctic storm"

"That's just one reason I like the snow
It also warms my limbs you know
I love it when it snows all night
It makes us all look clean and white"

Christmas party

I guess I am just a little bit tardy
I should have mentioned the Christmas party
The Natives always have a tree
It's for all the kids to see

John and Alice own the store
They have for twenty years or more
Jan told Alice "It's getting late
But Jack and I want to participate"

Alice told us what to wrap
What names to put on this or that
You can bet when we were finally done
There were several gifts for everyone

There was a large building used by all
It was the Church and the Community Hall
We set up a tree though it was a chore
They'd never had as big a tree before

They decorated it the old fashioned way
Doing it all took a whole extra day
They made popcorn into little balls
And hung paper chains around the walls

On Christmas Eve the moon was bright
We celebrated the birth of Christ
The party was enjoyed by all
I know the kids sure had a ball

On Christmas Day we were in the mood
To really dig in and enjoy the food
There were Kelp Pickles, salads fresh from the water
And any leftovers would be fed to the Otter

Many things gathered from the sea to eat
Cucumber, Urchin and something called Leek
There was stuffed Moose heart, pickled tongue too
And something that's called Moose nose stew

Platters of Venison and roast Beaver tails
And bread made of flour from dried Cattails
King Salmon heads made into soup
And wild potatoes that are a root

There were wild berries made into a sauce
And a salad made from some kind of Moss
There was fried Trout fresh from the brook
I tell you those ladies sure can cook

Sitka Spruce

I met a Sitka Spruce near 8 foot through
About as smart as any tree I ever knew
Except for the Redwoods along the south coast
Who, I think, probably know the most

I wrote down everything that Spruce said
And tried to decipher it while lying in bed
You would swear that tree was a thousand years old
You should hear all the stories that he can unfold

On Kodiak Island the Russians created a port
That's where they built their very first fort
The Russians were mean beyond a doubt
Several Native villages were wiped out

The Eskimos just couldn't comprehend
How there could be such terrible men
When the Eskimos finally had enough
The Russians found they too could be rough

He said "I thought Seward was a smart man
When he dealt the Russians out of the land
The Russians back then thought the deal was good
But now they'd undo it if only they could"

He said "I was glad your country made that deal
The Russians were killing too many Seal
I'm sure they didn't know about the gold
If they had they would never have sold"

"We trees alone are worth quite a lot
We're worth more than what they got
Some of us knew there was oil in the ground
But it took many a year for it to be found

He claimed to be a long distance communicator
That he talks to trees south of the equator
It's easy for him to talk to the southern coast
And the Sequoias are the tree he talks to the most

He talked to some Fir trees that sure made him wonder
Why some people think you could run out of lumber
The trees that need to be cut in Alaska alone
Would build every family in the States a new home

In just a few years, about eight or ten
You could do the same thing all over again
That's something I had often heard
So I have no reason to doubt his word

That tree said he liked it better at night
That sometimes the sun was just too bright
He said "I like to count the stars
Sometimes I can see Venus, Jupiter and Mars"

Leaving Alaska

Our time in Alaska was growing thin
All the men were out fishing again
We hadn't spent one night in my shack
We'll try to do that next time back

Next winter we are going to run the store
Be taking care of it for 3 months or more
Because Alice and John both need a rest
And John is scheduled for medical tests

We're looking forward to coming back here
So we leased the house for another year
That way we can leave some of our gear behind
And not have to ship it all again next time

Jim was flying in soon and we'd be on our way
To tell you the truth I wished I could stay
Living in Alaska can be a little rough
But living like we were, I couldn't get enough

We had a great time, the folks were so kind
More hospitable folks you'll just never find
Most all showed up to wish us good bye
I saw a little girl with a tear in her eye.

Homeward Bound

We stayed in Sitka over night
Catching the early morning flight
The sun light on the islands and the sea
Makes as beautiful a picture as you'll ever see

The early morning sun on the snow capped peaks
Casts blue shadows on the rivers and the creeks
The islands through the clouds makes quite a sight
We were still taking pictures at the end of our flight

We rented a car for the drive home
And before we left called Sal on the phone
We warned her we'd be a little late
She said "No worry I'll leave open the gate"

There was no more snow, spring was in the air
I felt like resting but knew I didn't dare
I needed to call Thor and let him know I was back
It was time once again to be a working Lumberjack

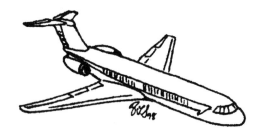

Plenty to do

Thor said he was glad I made it home
And asked how the weather was at Nome
I said "I really wouldn't know
But where we were it was twenty below"

"You see we were a ways west of Haines
Well south of the Wrangle Mountain Range
We got lots of rain and sometimes snow
And storms off the ocean, don't you know"

I asked him how things went down here
He said "You might just want to cheer
The tribe is going to take our advice
Because what we've done looks so nice"

He said "Things have sure been going on
The Enviros had to admit they were wrong
Some Politicians said they had never seen
A logged over area that was half as clean"

"This is something you'll like to hear
They've got work for us for 20 years
There's 20 more sections of timber land
And the Tribal Council wants us in command"

"But there is another thing that you should know
The EPA says the local mill has got to go
They say the mill is not only obsolete
No one needs a daily rate of a 100,000 feet"

"They say the smoke pollutes the air
And if closing it kills logging they don't care
The company which owns the mill
Plans to move its' business to Brazil"

"Now the Tribal Council wants us to make a plan
To help them build a mill on their land"
That was something I was glad to hear
I hoped it would also cut Veneer

We have to get started and work with haste
We want the mill to run with very little waste
We talked to the Tribal Chief, the leader of their clan
We needed to know more before we could make a plan

They needed a Planer and a Band Saw with an auto feed
I suggested a Peeler but that's not all they'll need
They needed to put in a pond and a Debarker too
But could get by without a Chipper for a year or two

It was going to cost a lot even for a small mill
The Tribe said not to worry they would foot the bill
We looked for bargains the best that we could
And kept the cost down as we said we would

The mill was built not far from town
On an area that was stable and sound
There was a large stream running near by
So the pond would have a water supply

We found a good man to lay out the mill
I'll have to admit we needed his skill
He planned it all to be easy to expand
It's a good thing they had plenty of land

With the big mill closing down come fall
We hired some men they didn't need at all
We were able to hire two good Millwrights
Because there was no more work at night

I spent that summer working on the mill
Taking advice from those who had the skill
I worked on the pond and built a canal
That was much easier than digging a well

Leveling the ground was quite a chore
I worked at that for a month or more
We finished several buildings by late fall
The next year we planned to finish them all

In the main building the equipment was new
And by fall we had it all assembled too
A lot of the works that wouldn't go to Brazil
Would be rebuilt and used in our mill

But at that time we didn't know
Which direction the wind would blow
The Mill Owners and the Tribe were working on a deal
If the rumors were right it would be a heck of a steal

We'd kept Rob logging and piling up stock
When the mill started running we'd need a lot
It turned out that Thor had plenty to do
Working in the shop and buying things new

Alaska Again

The first of November they closed the big mill
Started taking it down and shipping it to Brazil
What had to be done could be handled by Thor
So Jan and I flew to Alaska to run the store

About two months later I heard from Pilot Jim
His radio crackled and he said "I'm heading in
I've got some folks with me, we need to spend the night
It's mighty hard a flying when there isn't any light"

I said "I'm surprised, where are you at?"
"About two miles north of your old shack"
I really had to hurry to get lights on the dock
Jim came gliding in, though he couldn't see a lot

I asked him "What are you doing out in such a storm?"
He said "I'll tell you but let's get in where it's warm"
We went into the store, I turned up the heat
I asked Jan if she'd fix us something to eat

I told his passengers to take off their wraps
And hang them up on some empty racks
All the time those folks hadn't said a word
At least not one that I had heard

Then I invited them to find a chair
Looked up to find Thor standing there
Beside him stood his lovely wife
Never was I so surprised in my life

Of course my Jan was beside herself
Because they mean more to us than wealth
Pilot Jim sat there with a grin
While sipping at a glass of gin

I asked them how they liked their trip
They replied they enjoyed most of it
But the last few miles got a little rough
They could tell Jim sure knew his stuff

Jim said "I had to fly along the shore
But I've been in rougher spots before
We hit the wind and it slowed us down
And I couldn't even see the ground"

"I didn't want to take the chance
Of flying by the seat of my pants
So I took her up a thousand feet
And got above the rain and sleet"

"From there I could see all around
And knew exactly where to set her down
But I'm sure glad you set out the lights
It's tricky landing when it's dark at night"

I asked Jim to ride out the storm with us
He said he'd be pleased but "Don't let Jan make a fuss"
Thor and Jim can spin a good tale too
And between the three of us the lies sure flew

We invited some Natives into the store
And the stories were told by the score
I always thought that I could lie
But Jim and Thor sure passed me by

Some of the stories the Natives told
Made us want to go looking for gold
It took three days for the storm to break
When Jim took off, the bay was flat as a lake

In the weeks to come we had lots of fun
Went Salmon fishing and Thor caught one
I caught a Halibut the size of a barn door
Thor caught a small one, I wish he'd caught more

We did everything I had the year before
But together we did a whole lot more
They took a lot of pictures and we watched the Moose
They wanted to hear the stories of the Sitka Spruce

After about a month or so
Thor said it was time to go
He said "We'd love to stay a month or two
But there are too many things at home to do"

The next day I radioed Pilot Jim
And asked him when he'd be flying in
He said he had to fly to Glacier Bay
And was planning to stop by on the way

So if Thor could wait until next week
He'd fly them in to Sitka cheap
Thor told him that would be fine
They were ready to go any time

Back Home

Now we are back home too and I've gone to town
Jan and I are still trying to settle down
I've talked quite a lot to my friend by the well
And we both have a few more stories to tell

I also talked to my boys on the phone
They said they were sorry they couldn't get home
I haven't seen them since September last year
I miss them both and wish they were here

I called Thor on the phone
He was glad that we were home
He said "Things have been moving along quite fast
The Debarker's been running since week before last"

"The Planer is also set up and ready to go
But there's something else that you should know
The company that owned the big old mill
Took out what they wanted and moved to Brazil"

"They made us a deal that we couldn't turn down
And the contract keeps us safe and sound
We are to tear down what's left and they foot the bill
Whatever we want we can use in the new mill"

"The Council didn't know quite what to do
So they left that up to me and you
The Tribe's mill will be built cheap
And a share of the profits will be ours to keep"

I thought it was time to call Sawyer Rob
For over two years he's been on the job
He's willing to work both night and day
And I think it's time we raised his pay

Rob said "Things are going fine
Been building fence and running line
I'm sure you know I hired Bob
He's always said he likes this job"

We talked on the phone for an hour or more
He told me about the job I told him about the store
I said "I'll see you in a week or two
Thor has a job for me to do"

Back on the job

I drove to the job to look up Thor
Thought it was time to go to work once more
Thor said "There are things that I've left for you
I think you should hire a six man crew"

"Try to pick men that want to work in the mill
Willing to learn if they don't have the skill
I've hired all the skilled men that I could find
That's why we're ahead of schedule instead of behind"

"The pond sprung a leak but we got it sealed
And now it is full of logs that are peeled
That Rob sure is a very good man
He's sending in logs as fast as he can"

"He's been building fences and running lines
I guess he does that in between times
He's only running a three man crew
But they move logs like five men do"

I hired seven men but found only one that had skill
He had worked on the Head Rig in the big old mill
It didn't take long till we had everything running
And out on the Green Chain there was lumber a coming

We cut a hundred thousand feet the very first week
But we had more to do before the mill was complete
Thor had the men hired to finish the job
So we decided it better that I work with Rob

We are trying to develop a Timber Plantation
That plan will be better for the Indian Nation
I put in my time cutting brush and cleaning streams
It made it possible to fulfill some of my dreams

I cruised a lot of timber and marked trees to go
I had that job finished long before we had snow
I marked all the trees that should be cut
And tried not to miss any with rotten butts

One section of ground has a deep ravine
And in the bottom a beautiful stream
On it's sides the timber is thick
To log that timber would ruin the crick

If you built a road the land would slide
And ruin some places where the Deer reside
In another area the brush is thick
There's lots of Alder and Kinnikinnick

There are game trails going every where
All being used by Deer, Elk and Bear
It's a good area for them to hide
So we decided to set that section aside

A Cedar's Tale

Early one morning in the middle of the week
As I was marking timber along a creek
A Cedar said "I heard you can talk to trees
Would you take the time to talk to me"

The one thing he wanted most to know
Was why I hadn't marked him to go
I said "You're a healthy tree that's good and sound
And I'm not marking Cedar this time around"

"We'll be taking Cedar at a later time
Someday you'll be holding up a power line
But there is one thing that you should know
All those downed Cedar will have to go"

That Cedar seemed to understand
We were trying to help the land
He said "I have a story to tell you
My Dad told me so it must be true"

"About 20 miles to the west
There's a valley called the Eagle's Nest
It's surrounded with a high rocky rim
And there is only one way to get in"

"There a creek comes out of the wall
And creates a 100 foot water fall
At the base in the water spray
The Water Ouzels swim and play"

"And along the cliff's rocky crest
The Eagles build their nests
You can hear the Night Hawk's mating call
Above the sound of the water fall"

"There is a long meadow along the stream
All summer it stays lush and green
And in the meadow the birds do sing
The Meadowlark, Thrush and Red Wing"

"There are many Trout in the Beaver ponds
And most of the Does have two Fawns
You can see Otter most any day
It's one animal that loves to play"

"Dad said when his Dad was small
The valley burned in early fall
It's been over two hundred years since then
And the valley has grown to timber again"

"The birds, animals and fish are still there
The trees have grown large and as thick as hair
You can see Eagles soaring high over head
And hear the Eaglets screaming when they want fed"

"Years later when the valley was again green
Again there were Teepees to be seen
There was a beautiful lady with raven black hair
With her newlywed husband she was living there"

"When she was small she had lived with another tribe
She had been taken one day when her parents died
She lived a dozen years with the clan
Before she married a young man"

"She liked to swim in the cool clear water
She talked to the Deer and play with the Otter
She and her husband, who was very tall,
Spent much of their time at the waterfall"

"Dad said one night when the moon was pale
The newlyweds listened to the Coyote's wale
They sat by the fire till nearly midnight
When the moon went down the stars were bright"

"Suddenly she felt something was wrong
And what she felt was very strong
She said "I think we should move right away
We better move out as soon as it's day"

"Her husband said 'You could be right
We'll get our weapons and be ready to fight'
They went to the village and told them the same
And assured them they were not playing a game"

"The night was dark and they all hid
It's a good thing that they did
In about an hour though it seemed like more
The enemy came sneaking along the valley floor"

"The enemy were a bunch of Canadian Renegades
Who came south of the border making raids
It was the last surprise of their life
Many lives were saved by the tall Indian's wife"

I told him the Indian Nation owned the land
And I and their leader had talked of a plan
It's a beautiful valley so full of life
It ought to be a Park named for the wife

Surprise

We had six trailers parked along a stream
And worked hard to keep the campground clean
There were two Loggers camped further down
Both their wives worked jobs in town

Jan's and my trailer was a little small
I think it was the shortest of all
But that made it easy for Jan to clean
And left more time to fish the stream

Jan and I were ready to set down to eat,
When Sal drove in, looking quite neat
We welcomed her with open arms
And asked how things were on the farm

She said "Don't worry, everything's OK
And Sport's in the car, by the way"
I was sure glad to see my dog
As a pup I had gotten him from Rob

Sal said she'd talked to Tim the other day
He was at the ball park getting ready to play
He was laughing for with their names being Tim and Sam
The whole team was calling them Bim and Bam

Soon after that Rob drove in
He brought his wife and daughter Kim
Before I could ask about the job
Sal spoke up and asked "Where's Bob?"

Rob said "Bob's not far behind
He'll be driving in most any time"
There was one thing I sure didn't miss
When Bob came in Sal gave him a kiss

Bob hadn't been there very long
When he asked Sal "Is there something wrong"
She hesitated but then said "No
But I doubt if either of them know"

I asked them what they were talking about
That's when Bob pulled a diamond ring out
Sal said "Mom I don't want you to cry
Bob and I are getting married next July"

With that ring for all to see
Bob said "I hope you all agree"
I was surprised I have to admit
But Jan said she had suspected it

I said "The choice is really yours
Now Bob can help you with the chores"
I knew that I'd been had
Bob would soon call me Dad

There sure was alot of planning to do
I kidded Bob and Sal some too
I asked them "Why wait till July?"
And thought my Sal was going to cry

"I want my brothers there that day
While you of course give me away
So Bob and I have made a plan
And that time is best for Tim and Sam"

The Wedding

The wedding was held under the tree by the well
So now our friend the Fir has another story to tell
And some of the Cedars standing nearby
I swear like my wife they too did cry

The old well served as part of the alter
And I had to wear a suit to give away my daughter
But our friend the Fir tree said "Now that was fun
And you didn't lose a daughter you gained a son"

I had a good visit with Tim and Sam
I asked all about Bim's Grand Slam
Bam said "Most pitchers just can't hit the ball
Their time is spent working on throwing is all"

"But catchers are supposed to hit a ball real good
And Bim sure knows how to put a bat where he should"
I guess the boys both hit with power
Bam even hit one over the water tower

As pitchers they seem to be doing OK
They both won a game on the same day
They said they played a double header
And took turns catching for each other

Now I love baseball but I wasn't much good
I was always stoved up from cutting wood
I'm sure glad the twins could see the light
They'd rather play ball than work day and night

I quit working for Rob early that fall
To hunt and fish and have a ball
Thor says he enjoys running the job
But he's just filling in for our Boss Rob

Rob finally asked for time off to rest and play
So we gave him two months off but kept him on pay
I told him if he needed a few more
That he had earned another three or four

But we needed him back by early spring
By then we wanted to be in full swing
Though he said he'd like to play it by ear
He thought he'd be ready by the first of the year

Thoughts *by the* Brook

Quite often I set by the babbling brook
Working away at writing this book
Or walk through the timber for miles around
I've been talking to trees both rotten and sound

There are about half of the trees that beg to be cut
There are many things wrong including bad butts
There is no excuse for letting them stand
They do nothing but hinder the land

A beautiful forest is healthy and clean
Without dying timber or blow downs in streams
A healthy forest is something all can admire
It's not as apt to be blackened by fire

In places there are Wolves that may give you a scare
But don't worry about the Squirrels or the Hare
God made some dangerous animals to live on the land
But you must remember that he also made Man

If you think that the animals are mean or are cruel
Just remember they live by Mother Nature's rule
When you're out in the wilds keep that in mind
Play by her rules and you'll get along fine

The Bear

Now I don't want to cause anyone a scare
But I'd like to tell you about me and a Bear
When you go in the woods you best be prepared
Or you could end up in the hospital being repaired

Back about fifteen years ago
Early in fall before we had snow
It was a warm and sunshiny day
I didn't have time to dally away

I had promised Jan to paint the house
And to take the boys hunting for Grouse
I was on my back forty doing some scouting
When I heard a Fir tree that was really shouting

I asked him if he was shouting at me
He said "There is something you should see"
He asked me if I was afraid of a Bear
I said "A Grizzly might give me a scare"

He said "You see that big tree on the ground
The one the wind has finally blown down
It was old and hallow inside
The Squirrels used him to hide"

"They used him to make their home
As Bees filled him up with honey comb
They had to keep moving higher for their nests
For it seemed the Bees would never rest"

He said "I guess that everyone knows
That a Grizzly Bear has a very keen nose
That tree hadn't been down very long
When an old Grizzly Bear came along"

"Now that old Bear could smell the honey
And what he did next I thought was funny
A Bee must have stung him in the eye
Cause the Bear got mad and the bark did fly"

"The crack got wider, the honey did drip
But when the old Bear started licking it
His tongue got stuck in the crack
So he gave that tree a terrible whack"

"That was one irritated Bear
At the tree he sure did tear
He tore out a slab and he ate his fill
If he hadn't he'd be trying still"

The Fir tree said "I hear that stuff's worth money
You could get some buckets and fill them with honey
But be careful of that old Bear
Because he's standing just over there"

About that time the Bear let out a terrific roar
And I started making tracks 'cross the timber floor
Well, I thought, I have some money
I think I'll just buy my honey

When I saw him in the corner of my eye
I decided I better shift into high
I knew I'd have to set the pace
If I was going to win this race

In about two jumps I had doubled my speed
I was praying it would be all I'd need
I hoped I wouldn't run out of air
If I did he would have my hair

I have to admit I was in a rush
As I, then the Bear, hit the brush
So much hit him in the face
It's probably why I won that race

I jumped a fence that was five feet high
So now I know how it feels to fly
I was gaining speed at every jump
I thought that Bear was on my rump

While in the air I looked around
That old Bear was laying on the ground
The way he was rolling in the grass
I'm sure that he'd run out of gas

I went in the house and sat in a chair
I just couldn't seem to get enough air
I could barely breath and couldn't talk
I was so doggone weak I couldn't walk

After about an hour or so
I got up but was moving slow
I told my wife that Bear near did me in
I thought she'd be notifying the next of kin

I said "I'll give that Bear a chance
But we can't have him on the ranch
I have to protect the kids and you
So sharing this ranch just won't do"

I wanted to meet that Bear one on one
But next time with my trusty gun
I was home with Jan before sundown
And two days later I went to town

I needed to talk to the Warden about the Bear
And tell him that it nearly got my hair
He said "There's a lady I'd like to send out
I'd like you to show her all about"

That very night I got a phone call
She said her name was Rena Ball
She said "I am a Biologist from the zoo
And I want to have a word with you"

I told her in the morning the Warden would be out
And that would be a good time to show her about
Something in her tone alerted me
As to what her agenda just might be

She said my boys were telling all over town
How I had run a Grizzly Bear down
She said I should be ashamed
To kill a Bear that might be tamed

I said "My boys were just a little wrong
That Bear's not dead it's just long gone
And I didn't run him anywhere
I just plain out ran that Bear"

She said "There's something you should know
I know just how fast a Bear can go
A Bear can do sixty on a flat out run"
I said "I must have been doing sixty-one"

When the Warden arrived I showed them the ground
We hiked to the tree and looked all around
They went back to town seeming satisfied
I am sure they believed I hadn't lied

Mullan Tree

I took my dog Sport for a walk
I and a Spruce had a little talk
I had planned to go fishing in the brook
But wound up with another story for this book

The Spruce asked if I had heard of the Mullan Tree
I said "Yes, I'd read about it in history"
Captain Mullan surveyed a trail in 1854
Or maybe it was the year before

He and his men climbed a pass on the Fourth of July
It's called the Fourth of July Pass, now you know why
His men carved their names and the date in an old Pine
So their deeds would stay with us for a very long time

Later that trail was called a Military Road
I heard it was about as rough as a toad
And then the Mullan Road became it's name
And it extended west beyond Coeur d'Alene

It's name has been changed two times more
And instead of two lanes now it has four
There are signs put up for all to see
Be proud of John Mullan and the Mullan tree

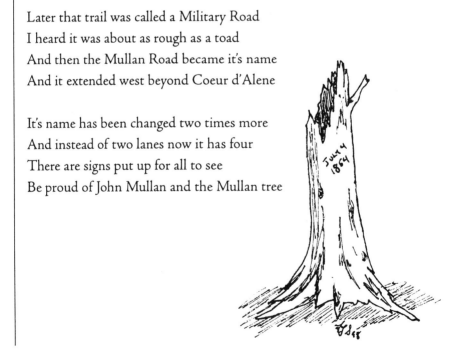

Sundance

I talked with an Alpine who lives high on a hill
He said the Sundance Fire sure gave him a thrill
But that fire should never have been
It went out of control due to careless men

It raced along at about twenty miles an hour
Everything in its' path it was quick to devour
If you're in a fire's path make no mistake
Either get out fast or get into a lake

We lost two good men in that holocaust
And were lucky there weren't many more lost
The Fire Spotter on Roman Nose survived that day
With a wet blanket over the cliff he made his way

In areas the fire was extremely hot
It burned the soil and melted rock
Now that was about thirty years ago
And it's healing itself but growing back slow

1910 Fire

All of the old trees remember when
There was that terrible fire in 1910
One tree told me he remembered it well
Some people lived by going down a well

That fire was bad for about six weeks
By the end of August it had reached it's peak
The loss wasn't measured by lumber back then
It was measured by the loss of a hundred men

By that time they'd built some rail
All along the old Mullan Trial
Also they had built the Milwaukee Line
With its high bridges it had taken time

The trains helped in the evacuation
In some of the towns it was a close situation
Those trains didn't just save people by the score
They saved them by the hundreds and more

Now War Eagle Tunnel is known quite well
It saved 34 men from a burning hell
Ranger Ed Pulaski showed them the way
Because of him they didn't die that day

39 men went in but only 34 came out alive
It's a wonder that any managed to survive
You can bet your hat it was hot in there
They lost some hide and lots of their hair

Ranger Pulaski had to fight
To control the panic during the night
Three men jumped him and one got away
He was found dead the very next day

They took Pulaski to check on his daughter and wife
Then to the hospital to save his life
From the heat and the smoke he was blind
But his sight returned in a few weeks time

Pulaski invented a tool that still bears his name
There's nothing quite like it in the fire fighting game
To build a fire trail, a saw and a shovel is what you need
But give me a Pulaski and I'll double the speed

Redwoods

There was one Redwood who talked rather slow
He said "You should have seen it a few thousand years ago
There were earthquakes up and down the coast
And in Mexico they shook the most"

"There always was some Mountain blowing its' top
And where lava flowed it got mighty hot
The Mountains quite often changed their shape
That's how we ended up with Crater Lake"

"Mt. Jefferson and the Three Sisters argued a lot
It seemed like one of them was always blowing its' top
And when Shasta and Bachelor joined the crowd
The noise they made got really loud"

He said "I'm sure that you have seen
Mt. Hood putting out a lot of steam
And it wasn't very many years ago
When Mt. St. Helens decided it would blow"

"Out west in the seventeen hundreds it began to change
Back when the Spanish started expanding their range
They lived several hundred miles south of here
Building Missions and settlements every year"

"We were Americans by the time
Of the Gold Rush back in Forty-nine
If the Spanish had had their way
We would be part of Mexico yet today"

He said "I remember back in Forty-Nine
When men from the east came west to mine
There were men of all ages from young to old
Who came out west just to hunt for gold"

"Some got rich and some didn't do so well
The majority just had a story to tell
Some of them stayed and made a new life
While others went home to their kids and wife"

If you think those Redwoods talk a little bold
Just remember they watched this nation unfold
They've seen man bring a lot of change
Now we have cities, farms and growing pains

Fruit trees

I have talked to fruit trees for many years
They have made me laugh till I shed tears
Take Apples, Peaches, Pears and Plums
They all talk with wobbly tongues

They say their tongues get the bends
I think they're fastened at both ends
They say they wobble to and fro
That's the way that fruit trees grow

They tell you when they're loaded with fruits
They'll need more water on their roots
They say they give more fruit that way
Than if you water with an overhead spray

Peaches will tell you they need lots of heat
If you want lots of Peaches and want them sweet
But too many people have been seen
Picking Peaches when they're too green

Plums you can wait till early fall
Just shake the tree and they'll fall
We grow Apples from coast to coast
Of all fruit trees they're planted the most

One tree said his great grand tree came
Out from St. Louis by Wagon Train
He said he got so dog gone dry
He thought for sure he was going to die

He said he came out in 1861
And it sure was hot in the summer sun
They loaded one wagon with the very best
To plant them all out here in the west

He said the wagon was loaded from front to back
They were standing upright but sure were packed
Often there wasn't enough water to go around
But one time crossing a river he nearly drowned

They were set in containers on the wagon floor
But even at that his roots got sore
A few trees were stolen along the way
He hoped they were planted and were doing OK

They made the trip and most survived
And that orchard really thrived
"Grandpa was grown from just a seed
But I was grafted so I guess I'm pedigreed"

A Cherry has a beautiful bloom
I like the smell of Cherry perfume
And along about the first of July
I can make myself a Cherry pie

I've tried many times to talk to a Cherry tree
But I've never known one that would speak to me
No matter how I've tried and tried
My guess is their tongues are tied

A Walnut tree makes wonderful shade
It's nuts can be as big as an egg
I wonder about that nut with the English name
Was he brought over here from England or Spain

I met a tree with a southern drawl
And in every sentence there was a you-all
He said his folks came from down San Antonio way
And he could remember one March day

On that day the old Mission fell
It left no one to ring the bell
When Travis, Bowie and Crocket made their stand
And gave their blood for Texas land

It's Hard to Kill a tree

One tree said "You can't kill a tree
Because all our seed are part of we
Oh sure you can cut me down
Scatter my wood all over town"

"You could burn me up in a fire place
But that doesn't mean I'm out of the race
A strong enough wind might tear me down
It could rip my roots right out of the ground"

"But that wouldn't be the end of me
My seed would sprout and I'd be another tree
Oh sure my limbs and needles and wood might die
But all of my off spring and seeds are part of I"

That's why a tree says he's hard to kill
Because part of him will be here still
It's funny I hadn't thought of if that way
But God put trees here and meant them to stay

A tree's faith is different than yours or mine
He'll be here as long as there is time
Life and time is something we must earn
Reading the Good Book is one way to learn

My friend the Fir by the well
Expressed it all very well
This is what he had to say
"Follow God's foot steps every day"

A Maple Tree

A Maple tree sprouted along our north wall
Before I knew it was four feet tall
I said that tree has to come out of there
Sal said she'd transplant it and she knew where

She planted it near the Septic Tank's overflow
And you ought to have seen that tree grow
It's forty feet high and twenty feet wide
Sal says that tree is her joy and pride

It grows in our lawn all bordered with flowers
We have set in it's shade for many hours
And though it seems a little shy
It does converse with Sal and I

I trim that tree most every year
It's grown into a giant sphere
You ought to see it in the fall
In colors it tries to out do them all

I've seen many a Deer give birth to a Fawn
In the shade of the Maple out on our lawn
And Sport will play with all the Deer
But he doesn't let the Coyotes near

And we have an orchard that's doing good
On an acre of ground where the old barn stood
We enjoy watching Deer that come there to play
We taught our dog Sport to keep the Moose away

One time the Maple tree let out a shout
The neighbors fence was down, his Cows were out
My wife called the neighbors on the phone
But as luck would have it no one was home

I took Jan and Sport and away we went
And herded those Cows back through the fence
We worked on the fence for an hour or more
And built it back stronger than it was before

An old Bull Moose had tore the fence down
I hoped he wasn't still hanging around
I wouldn't have to use my gun
Sport would put him on the run

I've seen Sport and that Bull go round and round
I thought Sport would be trampled into the ground
But old Sport is mighty smart for a Dog
I've seen him worry that Bull out in the bog

And there he let that old Moose stand
That's the way Sport had it planned
It took awhile for the Moose to work free
When he did it was a joy to see

He has been getting meaner every year
He's become an animal that one should fear
That Moose would make a lot of good meat
Non-Hunters will tell you it's not fit to eat

They say to leave him for the Wolves to kill
That way the Antis can have a thrill
Of course if that Old Bull should die
It sure would make those poor guys cry

They took a Pledge

One of the "Anti Clubs" held a meeting last fall
Forest Rangers and Loggers were invited, one and all
So some of us Lumberjacks decided we should
Try to get to that meeting if we could

Two hundred seats were filled in record time
Quite a few of those men were friends of mine
But there were Tree Huggers, Enviros and Politicians too
And I mean there was more than just a few

They introduced the first man as Speaker of the House
The first thing he did was call every Logger a Louse
I guess you know that didn't sit too well
Some of the Loggers wanted to ring his bell

He said "We're here to close the woods down
So you better start looking for jobs in town"
He said "We now have a lot more clout"
He was talking about Politicians no doubt

He rattled on for half an hour or more
And then another guy took the floor
I thought he was as rough as the first
But some men thought he was the worst

He said "No one should cut a tree
God put them here for us to see
If you cut one down the land will flood
And all the water will turn to mud"

"Cutting trees is something we should do without"
You should have heard the Tree-Huggers cheer and shout
He said "Friends the logging has got to stop"
But in my opinion he didn't know a lot

Several more guys had their say
They rattled on for half a day
Then a Politician took the floor
He made the mistake of calling on Thor

Now Thor got up and then so did I
With two dozen Jacks standing by
It looked as if there might be a fight
But Thor knew what to say and said it right

This is the way he started his speech
And I admit I thought it was neat
"For over three hours you've given us hell
But now there's something I'm going to tell"

"For every old tree that should come down
There's several young trees standing around
Every tree that's removed from the forest floor
Will leave the room for three or four"

"How many of you men don't want a tree cut?"
There were dozens of hands shot right up
"You are saying we are wrong and you are right
I challenge you to start proving it tonight"

"We expect you to set the example to show us the way
So you'll be living without wood starting today
I doubt if I can live without wood
But you are saying everyone should"

"Here are the rules for you to go by
So read them all before you try
Sign the pledge before you go out the door
You'll use no wood for 30 days or more"

"There'll be no rolls of paper hanging on the wall
In fact there'll be no paper at all
That's just the first of what you'll do without
It's going to be rough I have no doubt"

"For you can't stay under your roof tonight
No wood for rafters would be quite a sight
Phones and electricity will be off limits too
Because without poles no juice would go through"

"Here's a list of the things you must do without
In a month we'll see if you still cheer and shout
There are things made of wood not on this list
It's up to your conscious to catch what's been missed"

That was what Thor had to say
And suggested a meeting in thirty days
There were twenty men that signed the pledge
The rest of the Antis just hung their heads

At the next meeting only eight men came in
And they were all looking mighty grim
Not one of the eight had stuck it out
They learned wood products we can't do without

Without rolls of toilet paper on the wall
One guy couldn't stand to try at all
One teacher showed up at the end
Without books he wasn't able to begin

All of them said it couldn't be done
At least not the way our world is run
I heard there were several other men
Who said they wouldn't want to try that again

The Ranger admitted that Thor was right
That his idea had deferred a fight
It's been proven that people must have wood
With selective logging they can have what they should

My Friend's Wish

My friend by the well seems healthy and strong
But he says he feels that something is wrong
Though he's only ninety years old
Much of the time he feels too cold

He says his hearing is not up to par
And he no longer can see very far
He said "This is what I want you to do
And I hope I won't have to argue with you"

"I know you don't need a new house or a barn
But promise you'll use me here on the farm
Treat my offspring like you've treated me
And they'll be as happy as trees can be"

"I want you to cut me before too long
While my wood is still good and strong
Make some of me into a coffin and lay me aside
So I can hold you when you too have died"

"Carve your families' names on one of my boards
Because you're the ones that I've adored"
Though his spark may be getting dim
He's not ready yet to be cashed in

I've loved that tree for many years
When he goes I know there will be tears
When his time has come to go
He'll be the one to let me know

Tree Talk

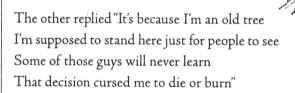

I heard two trees talking the other day
And this is what I heard one say
He said "Pete, I know not why
You're doomed to stand here and die"

"They took your sons and left you stand
Why was that decision made by man?
I know you're old and want to be cut
And I know you've got a rotten butt"

The other replied "It's because I'm an old tree
I'm supposed to stand here just for people to see
Some of those guys will never learn
That decision cursed me to die or burn"

"I'm going to fall right in that stream
And then you'll hear the people scream
You see they wont dare to take me out
That would muddy the water and kill some Trout"

"Selective logging would have been the way to go
By experienced Loggers, guys that really know
To have left my sons to grow would have been wise
In thirty more years they would have doubled their size"

"Now thirty years isn't very long
But chances are by then I'll be gone
I wish people would think and keep in mind
My sons would have become old growth if given time"

My Stream

I own a couple miles of stream
And try to keep it clear and clean
But the Moose and Elk and Deer and Bear
Will go to the bathroom anywhere

The Coon and Beaver and Skunk and Mink
Don't give a hoot where they stink
But let one of my Cows get near the stream
And you can bet some one will scream

A person can't do much on their farm
Without someone, somewhere claiming harm
One day a Beaver fell a tree across my stream
And I thought I could remove it without being seen

I removed the tree and played with the Otter
Might have gotten a little dirt in the water
In about a week I got word by mail
I was to pay a fine or go to jail

Someone far away says they can
Do a better job of managing my land
I checked on the Beaver just last week
Now they have a dam built across the creek

They can flood my land, I'm not allowed to care
The wild Ducks and Geese will be living there
Of course all the flooded trees will die
And some Environmentalists will wonder why

They don't seem to know that flooding land
Will kill a healthy timber stand
Then they'll say the Beaver have to go
And I will say "I told you so"

The ponds will dry up and lower the stream
Then the Environmentalists will really scream
All this because a Beaver fell a tree
And the Law said the harm was caused by me

Pend Orielle

High on a mountain near the timber line
I set on a rock 'neath a White Bark Pine
Spending some hours watching the Deer, Elk and Bear
Taking pictures of the animals living up there

That old tree sure knows the score
He says his age is Ninety-Four
He says a Moose once broke off a limb
And many is the Martin who played on him

He can see most of lake Pend Oreille
And vehicles running on the old highway
In clouds or when the sun shines through
That Pine tree has a beautiful view

When he was little he learned stories that were old
And he had a tale he thought I should be told
Years ago Indians lived on Pend Orielle lake
They were good people make no mistake

Thompson plied the Clarks' Fork river one day
Arriving at the lake in the month of May
He built a house and opened for trade
Wonder if he knew the history he made

With the house went a lot of pride
He named it for the Kallispell tribe
The house is gone but we remember today
Many have followed but he led the way

The Deer Yard

I'm always concerned in the fall of the year
Will Mother Nature be hard on the Elk and the Deer
I know of one river bottom a half a mile wide
It's a natural place for game to hide

There grow many a tree of the deciduous kind
Also many species of the needled Pine
Along the river the brush is thick
There's Aspen and Alder and Kinnikinnick

The Beaver love the Aspen best of all
They start storing for winter in early fall
They fall many trees and chew off the limbs
And that's when their work really begins

They build houses of limbs and work in the dark
Then they'll live all winter on limbs and bark
You'll never see them out in a cold winter storm
But they may fall some trees if the winter is warm

Deer will head to the low land along some creek
Where there's plenty of water and brush to eat
They like the buds from the Aspen trees
But they'll also eat Alder bark and leaves

One winter came early a few years ago
I remember it well because of the snow
In the bottom land where there is good feeding ground
Deer by the hundreds moved in from miles around

The way it was snowing the Deer would have it hard
So I went to take a look at the wintering yard
I could see that too soon the Deer would need help
Before the winter was over so would the Elk

So I talked to a Warden, the man in command
He said he would have to look over the land
He said he'd call me in a week or two
Someday when he had nothing important to do

Finally on New Year's Day we flew over the yard
Anyone could see the Deer were having it hard
But the Officer said that the Deer looked OK
Policy was to starve them rather than feed them hay

That wasn't what I had in mind
The yard had food of the natural kind
But the snow was nearly eight feet deep
The Deer were stranded, couldn't reach it to eat

If people built trails and packed down the snow
The Deer would have more places to go
The Warden said he didn't think it was too smart
He'd just starve off the Deer and get a new start

I talked to four Loggers who lived near by
None of those men wanted the Deer to die
But the Officer had made it clear
There was no budget to feed the Deer

We decided to pass the word
We needed help to save the herd
I knew I could count on Rob and Thor
They had helped me save Deer before

We started making plans that very day
With lots of help from a Logger named Jay
He had a Skidder and a Dozer larger than mine
And he was out of work so he had the time

We moved into the Deer yard the very next day
And two more Skidders were on their way
The snow in the yard was nearly eight feet deep
We soon found Deer that were hungry and weak

I fell some Birch that were growing near
Stripped off the branches to feed the Deer
There were Deer just standing or laying all around
With several feet of snow between them and the ground

The Dozers moved along very slow
In many places they just couldn't go
The Skidders were having a harder time
Often pulling themselves by their skidding line

I had help feeding Deer the following day
And more help was coming from farther away
Two more Skidders arrived for the job
Then Thor showed up and so did Rob

While Rob went back into town
To get enough feed to go around
Thor donned snow shoes to look on ahead
He saw hundreds of Deer but found only one dead

That Deer had been killed by a Mountain Lion
They have to eat or they too would be dyin'
Every day there were Deer killed by the Cats
And every day the new snow covered the tracks

Snowmobilers started showing up every day
We finally had to start turning some away
There were snowmobiles running every where
And some of those guys didn't seem to care

They would run over a Deer or drive on past
More interested in racing around fast
Those were the kind of guys that we let go
All they wanted to do was play in the snow

But there were many that did a good job
They packed down the trails working with Rob
Hauled water and pellets to stranded Deer
They even hauled in brush if none was near

The Dozers and Skidders were doing it right
They worked all day and half of the night
Whenever a Skidder would get bogged in the snow
A Dozer would be called and pull it out slow

Water is one thing Deer really need
They need even more with Pellet Feed
We planned to feed pellets for a month or more
The Dozers cleared snow from the river's shore

In about a week the job was nearly done
It stopped snowing we could see the sun
The clouds cleared away and it turned cold at night
We planned to patrol the yard for about a fortnight

Around that time a copter came in flying slow
The pilot set it down on the hard packed snow
I thought for a minute that they were lost
It couldn't be Wardens' because of the cost

Well that just goes to show that I can be wrong
It was the Conservation Officer with a Warden along
The Officer said he wanted to talk
I asked him if he'd like to take a walk

"No," he said "I want you all to hear
You did a great job of saving the Deer
But over the ridge is a yard full of Elk
Those animals now are in need of help"

"The hills are steep along the river's far side
And the snow on the hills has started to slide
The snow filled the river and its packed in hard
So now the river is flooding the whole Elk yard"

Thor and I rode in the copter and had us a look
It was plain to see we needed a good Chinook
Something had to be done and done very fast
Or the Elk would have water right up to their _ _ _

The Officer said they'd pay if we took the job
I wondered if the State had found a bank to rob
Thor thought it would cost at least thirty grand
We'd have to blast, and open more grazing land

The Officer said "I'll have to think"
I said "You have as long it takes to blink
Because we have to know mighty fast
Wait too long and Elk won't last"

He said "Start the Dozers on their way
We'll sign your orders yet today"
The Dozers and Skidders worked all night
They were on top of the ridge by daylight

Thor and I went in to town
We picked up our orders and looked around
Found a Helicopter that would do the job
But knew we also needed help from Rob

We knew we needed to work fast
By daylight we wanted to blast
The snow slide had damned the river up tight
And blasting was needed to open it right

We lowered the dynamite onto the Jam below
And asked Rob if he was ready to go
Rob turned pale and I thought he'd refuse
But he said "Someone has got to light the fuse"

We lowered Rob onto the hard packed snow
Once he lit the fuse he was ready to go
But there was plenty of time to pull him back up
Before the twenty foot fuse burned to make it erupt

The copter sat on the ridge with all of its crew
Waiting to watch when the Dynamite blew
The powder went off with a great roar
We were told it was heard ten miles or more

Thor watched through a pair of binocs
He said he could see flying rocks
The Elk sure were scared but had no place to go
Some of them tried and were stuck in the snow

The blast opened the channel so the water flowed free
And the Elk down below us were a pleasure to see
The water in the Elk yard was soon to go down
And not one of the Elk did we find drowned

There were too many animals for that one yard
And to move some out proved to be rather hard
The weather turned colder and the wind turned raw
We had to drive some into a large timbered draw

We built a trail up and over the ridge
In one place we had to build a snow bridge
We needed a corral that would hold lots of hay
That job was turned over to the Logger named Jay

The corral was built of small Jack Pine
And Jay put it up in record time
That's when the Skidders really earned their pay
They skidded corral poles fighting snow all the way

Two Snow Cats and two Skidders stayed on the job
Under the direction of Jay and Rob
Two men with snowmobiles volunteered to stay
To keep trails packed and scatter out hay

It was God's blessing that we had so much help
And the men would get paid for helping the Elk
I intended to see what I could do
To get some pay for the rest of the crew

In about two weeks I got a call from Rob
He said he wished I'd come out to the job
He said "I sure need some help
There are too many Lions feeding on Elk"

"They are also killing too many Deer
That's only one of the reasons I need you here"
I contacted the Warden and went out the next morn
Though the Weather Man had predicted another storm

There were too many Elk and Deer already killed
About a dozen Cougars had their bellies filled
The Warden said "This will never do
We'll have to live trap one or two"

I suggested shooting three or four
And then trapping out a couple more
You see two big Cats is all you need
Or by spring we'd have no game to feed

Most of the Cats were a little shy
They moved from the trails to let us go by
But there was one old Cougar who sat on a limb
Snarling and waiting to do one of us in

Now that old Cat is a rug on my floor
And he won't be killing Elk any more
A pair of Cougars we left alone
That area they've made their home

The rest of the Cats were tranquilized
And blinders were taped over their eyes
We muzzled them so they couldn't bite
And tied up their feet good and tight

Now two of those Cats are in a zoo
A pair are over in Europe too
The others were released and again hunt Deer
But their doing it many miles from here

As Winter progressed and Spring grew near
The men kept busy taking care of the Deer
The first week of March came a real Chinook
I'd say the snow settled a good three foot

Late in March things were going quite well
When we found several Moose in the hay corral
It didn't matter it was about out of hay
And soon we were going to stop feeding any way

We took down the corral and pulled all the nails
And spent one day just skidding out the rails
The men with the Snow Cats sure did a good job
And the Skidders were moved out by Jay and our Rob

There were animals lost that was for sure
But many other areas lost a lot more
Since then the herds have grown back both Deer and Elk
And I give all the credit to all those who helped

Seen Not Used

You say trees are to be seen not used
I find that statement has me confused
There are thousands of things made out of wood
We can make them forever if we replant as we should

Some people burn wood to keep themselves warm
What would they do in a cold winter storm
Many houses have wooden walls and hardwood floors
You see docks built of wood along the lake shores

Across our nation run railroads
On wooden ties they carry heavy loads
Without the ties there would be no rails
We'd be crossing the country on wagon trails

There was a Sherwood forest and a Robin Hood
His bows and arrows were made of wood
When Columbus sailed the ocean blue
His ships were made of lumber too

The Pilgrims may have landed on Plymouth Rock
But to unload they had to build a dock
For hearth and home trees had to fall
Only the Indian's help let them survive at all

We've all heard of Birch Bark canoes
In places that was all folks had to use
When Lewis and Clark needed a boat
They hollowed out a log so it would float

Where would that rascal Tom Sawyer be
Without a picket fence or a raft made from a tree
Without a bat there would be no baseball
Nor a Mantle or Ruth to inspire us all

There were many golden treasures in King Tut's tomb
But there was also wood that furnished the room
Vikings in Long Boats once ruled the waves
There were even wooden clubs back in the caves

God asked Noah to build an Ark
He used good wood not the bark
It had to be a very strong boat
Very large but yet would float

Noah and his sons laid out a plan
They built the Ark over a hundred year span
That old Ark would be a pleasure to see
You can bet they used thousands of trees

Noah was a much better man than you or me
He fathered a son when he was five hundred and three
And then he fathered a couple more
After the age of five hundred and four

Now when I wake up the first thing I see
Is a wooden beamed ceiling looking back at me
Books on a shelf and pictures on a the wall
A walnut dresser and an oak stand in the hall

God put trees here and I think he did good
I speak for myself when I say I'll use wood
But I feel he gave us the responsibilities
To use his gifts wisely and replant the trees

End

My friend the Fir tree down by the well
Has been gone now for quite a spell
His off spring of all ages are growing all around
And millions of his seeds are still in the ground

Some of his sons and daughters are 60 years old
They too can tell stories and talk quite bold
And since that tree was so very dear to me
I'll leave them grow for my grand kids to see